Droughts

WITNESS TO DISASTER

"When the Well's dry, we
know the Worth of Water."

– Benjamin Franklin,
from *Poor Richard's Almanac* of 1746

Created in the 1930s when Hoover Dam was built, Lake Mead covers 110 miles
of the Colorado River. It provides water for nearly 25 million people, including the
residents of Las Vegas, Los Angeles, and San Diego. Because of overuse and
prolonged drought in the Southwest, in 2008 Lake Mead was at half capacity.

Droughts

WITNESS TO DISASTER

JUDY & DENNIS FRADIN

NATIONAL GEOGRAPHIC

WASHINGTON, D.C.

Text copyright © 2008 Judith Bloom Fradin and Dennis Brindell Fradin

Founded in 1888, the National Geographic Society is one of the largest nonprofit scientific and educational organizations in the world. It reaches more than 285 million people worldwide each month through its official journal, NATIONAL GEOGRAPHIC, and its four other magazines; the National Geographic Channel; television documentaries; radio programs; films; books; videos and DVDs; maps; and interactive media. National Geographic has funded more than 8,000 scientific research projects and supports an education program combating geographic illiteracy.

For more information, please call 1-800-NGS-LINE (647-5463) or write to the following address:
National Geographic Society
1145 17th Street N.W.
Washington, D.C. 20036-4688
U.S.A.

Visit us online at www.nationalgeographic.com/books

For information about special discounts for bulk purchases, please contact National Geographic Books Special Sales at ngspecsales@ngs.org

For rights or permissions inquiries, please contact National Geographic Books Subsidiary Rights: ngbookrights@ngs.org

Fradin, Judith Bloom.
 Droughts / Judy and Dennis Fradin.
   p. cm. -- (Witness to disaster)
 Includes bibliographical references and index.
 ISBN 978-1-4263-0339-5 (hardcover : alk. paper) -- ISBN 978-1-4263-0340-1 (library binding : alk. paper)
 1. Droughts--Juvenile literature. I. Fradin, Dennis B. II. Title.
 QC929.25.F73 2008
 363.34'929--dc22
                                    2008020424

Hardcover ISBN: 978-1-4263-0339-5
Library Edition ISBN: 978-1-4263-0340-1
Printed in the United States

Series design by Daniel Banks, Project Design Company; Designer, Kerri Sarembock, Project Design Company

The body text is set in Meridien
The display text is set in ITC Franklin Gothic

National Geographic Society
John M. Fahey, Jr., President and Chief Executive Officer
Gilbert M. Grosvenor, Chairman of the Board
Tim T. Kelly, President, Global Media Group
John Q. Griffin, President, Publishing
Nina D. Hoffman, Executive Vice President; President, Book Publishing Group

Staff for This Book
Nancy Laties Feresten, Vice President, Editor-in-Chief of Children's Books
Amy Shields, Executive Editor
Bea Jackson, Director of Design and Illustration
Jim Hiscott, Art Director
Lori Epstein, Illustrations Editor
Jean Cantu, Illustrations Specialist
Carl Mehler, Director of Maps
Jennifer A. Thornton, Managing Editor
Priyanka Lamichhane, Assistant Editor
R. Gary Colbert, Production Director
Lewis R. Bassford, Production Manager
Rachel Faulise, Nicole Elliott, Manufacturing Managers

CONTENTS

Madagascar, the world's fourth largest island, lies off the southeast
coast of Africa. The south end of the island nation is plagued by
droughts. Islanders walk to work through choking dust.

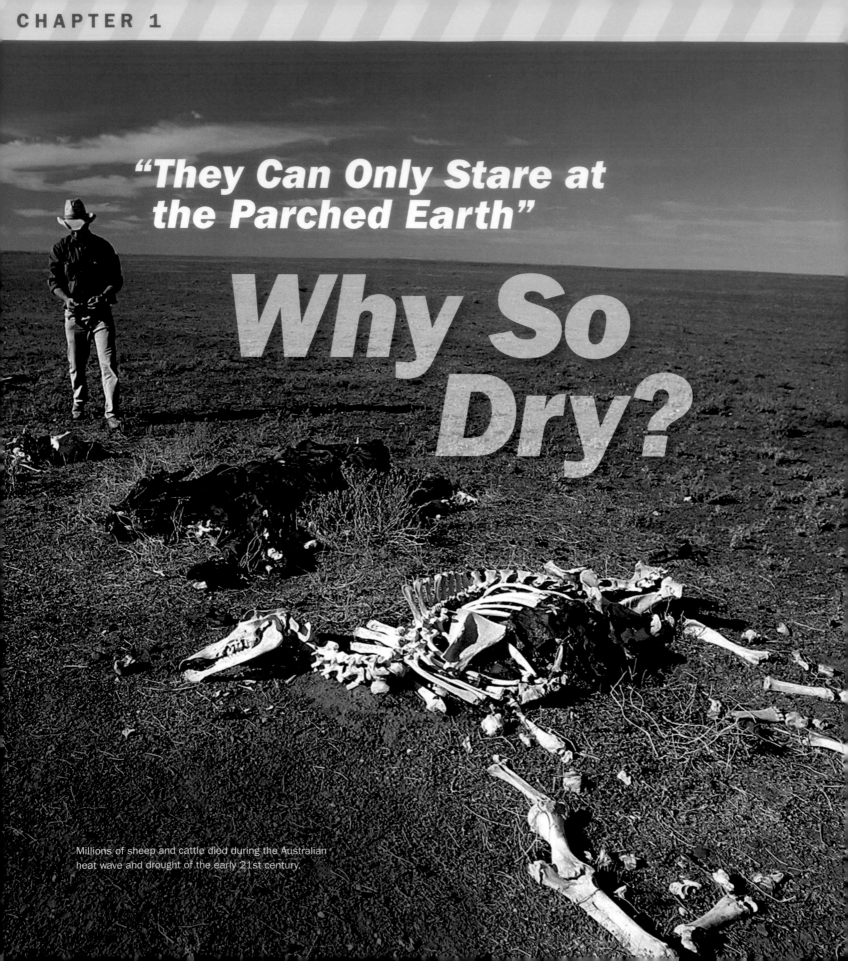

CHAPTER 1

"They Can Only Stare at the Parched Earth"

Why So Dry?

Millions of sheep and cattle died during the Australian heat wave and drought of the early 21st century.

"Lots of dust, dirt, no water, no grass, hot, millions of grasshoppers just eating anything, lots of kangaroos looking for food, the ground was so hard..."

Pippa Smith, describing the Australian drought of the early 2000s

Praying for rain in drought-stricken India

The inhabitants of Rajpar, India, were desperate for water. During periods of ample rainfall, villagers lowered buckets a short way down Rajpar's big well, then pulled up the water-filled containers. In the year 2000, however, due to a long dry spell, the well contained only a barely visible puddle at the bottom. To get it, villagers lowered a volunteer down the well with ropes.

Deeper and deeper she went: 50 feet, 100 feet, 150 feet, and finally 200 feet below ground level. There—20 stories beneath the Earth's surface— she filled containers with water from the bottom of the well. She was then pulled up to the surface, where she distributed the precious liquid to her neighbors.

At the time, India was suffering from a prolonged dry period known as a *drought*. With temperatures sizzling at about 110°F, heatstroke claimed many victims. Crops withered and died, leaving some people with nothing to eat but grass.

"In village after village, hunger stalks men, women, and children," declared Atal Behari Vajpayee, India's Prime Minister. "More than 50 million people have been affected by the drought. They can only stare at the parched

The worst drought in decades sparked dozens of wildfires in Portugal and Spain on August 22, 2005. About 600,000 acres (close to a thousand square miles) of woodlands were destroyed.

earth and hope that this year the monsoons [rains] will not elude them."

Intense droughts struck every continent except Antarctica in the first decade of the 21st century. By 2008 the drought in China was so severe that the massive Yangtze River was at its shallowest in at least 142 years, stranding dozens of ships. Spain, Portugal, and France were among Europe's hardest hit countries.

Besides crop failures and water shortages, the European droughts triggered another kind of natural disaster: wildfires. Thousands of forest fires blazed across Europe in the first decade of the new millennium. By July 2005, wildfires had destroyed or damaged hundreds of square miles of forests.

In Africa, no nation has suffered from drought more than Ethiopia. Ethiopian droughts often result in famines—periods of extreme food shortages during which large numbers of people starve.

Drought struck Ethiopia again in 2002. "God willing, the rains will come and we will grow something," said Melike Temamo, an Ethiopian woman. Sadly, by the time the drought-related famine ended in 2003, thousands of Ethiopians, including Melike's four-year-old child, had died. Were it not for food and water sent by other nations and by relief agencies, millions more might have died.

Australia, a country that is also a continent, is very dry even in normal times. In fact, roughly a third of Australia is desert. Starting in 2002, Australia was struck by its worst drought in a century. Called the "Big Dry," this drought was still going strong in early 2008, when 70% of Australia was suffering from abnormally dry conditions.

The Big Dry left people without enough water to drink. Toowoomba, a city of 100,000 in eastern Australia, considered using recycled sewage for part of its drinking water supply. Although the water would have been treated

"Helicopter cowboys" herd Australia's wild camels into corrals in order to protect crops from the hungry animals.

and cleaned and scientists said it would be safe to drink, Toowoomba residents rejected the plan. The "yuk factor" decided the vote, as people didn't want to drink water that had recently gone down someone's toilet or sink.

The Big Dry also took its toll on wildlife. Thirst and hunger drove kangaroos into urban areas including Canberra, Australia's capital. Australia is also home to more wild camels than any other country. These animals, famous for being able to go long periods without drinking, became so thirsty that they too began to invade populated areas.

Meanwhile, one of South America's most disastrous dry spells was devastating the state of Amazonas in Brazil. Roughly the size of Alaska, Amazonas contains parts of two natural treasures: the Amazon River and the Amazon Rain Forest.

As the Amazon and other rivers and lakes in the area shrank, people walked and rode bicycles where boats were once the only means of travel. Thirsty people drank polluted water and became ill. Medicine, fresh water, and food could not reach them because boats could not get through.

"The drought turns green to yellow, and yellow to brown. The dust rises on the wind, colors the sky, and generates intense earthy smells when rain beckons but does not fall. Crops wither, livestock die, and water feels so precious that you're tuned in to every drop."

Climatologist **James Risbey**, describing Australia's "Big Dry"

WITNESS TO A DROUGHT

"We have five children, ranging in age from ten to one. Since the drought began in 2002, drought might be all that some of them remember. The children know that they cannot have a bath every day. Their bath is only about four inches high. If they have a shower, it is for three minutes only and we use an egg timer. When they clean their teeth we make sure the tap is turned off in-between and the water does not run the whole time. I guess we as a family have grown up with the drought."

Pippa Smith, describing how Australia's water shortage has affected her family

A jar under a water fountain in this Australian school captures water that would otherwise go down the drain.

Wildfires broke out in the Amazon Rain Forest, destroying large numbers of trees. Data gathered by spacecraft high above Earth revealed more bad news. Smoke from the forest fires interfered with the formation of rain clouds that might have relieved the drought.

The western United States was one of North America's drought "hot spots." As of early 2008, Arizona was entering its 14th straight year of drought. Utah, Idaho, California, and Washington were among the other drought-stricken western states.

By 2004 California's Lake Arrowhead was at its lowest level ever measured. From July 2006 to May 2007 downtown Los Angeles received less than four inches of rain—one-fourth its usual amount and less than some deserts receive over the same time period. Rattlesnakes came down from southern California hills and became backyard hazards. The rattlers were chasing their prey—small animals that wandered into residential areas in search of water.

The great western drought changed the landscape. The water level in Lake Powell, located in Utah and Arizona, fell so low that previously unseen islands appeared. By 2004 the country's largest artificial body of water,

Lake Mead at the Nevada-Arizona border, had dropped about 100 feet. The water was so low that St. Thomas, Nevada, an old ghost town buried beneath the lake, was uncovered. In 2008 scientists predicted that, partly due to drought, Lake Mead may be totally dry by 2021. This is disturbing news for millions of people who receive water from Lake Mead, including residents of Las Vegas, Nevada, and Los Angeles and San Diego, California.

Other parts of the U.S. were also suffering. By fall of 2007 more than a quarter of the Southeast was in the grip of an "exceptional" drought—the National Weather Service's term for the worst dry spells. States afflicted by terrible drought included Georgia, Alabama, Tennessee, North Carolina, South Carolina, Virginia, and Kentucky.

In the northern half of Georgia, water was so precious that nearly all outside lawn and garden watering was banned. Officials warned that Lake Lanier, the main source of water for the people of Atlanta, Georgia, was in danger of disappearing altogether. In North Carolina, officials recommended that people wash their clothes by wearing them in the shower because water was at such a premium.

Taken as a whole, 55 percent of the United States was experiencing abnormally dry or drought conditions by early 2008. With unusually dry weather afflicting so many places around the world, people wanted to know: What was causing all these droughts?

In 2006-2007, Florida suffered one of the worst droughts in its history. The water in Lake Okeechobee fell to record low levels. No boats could dock at this pier!

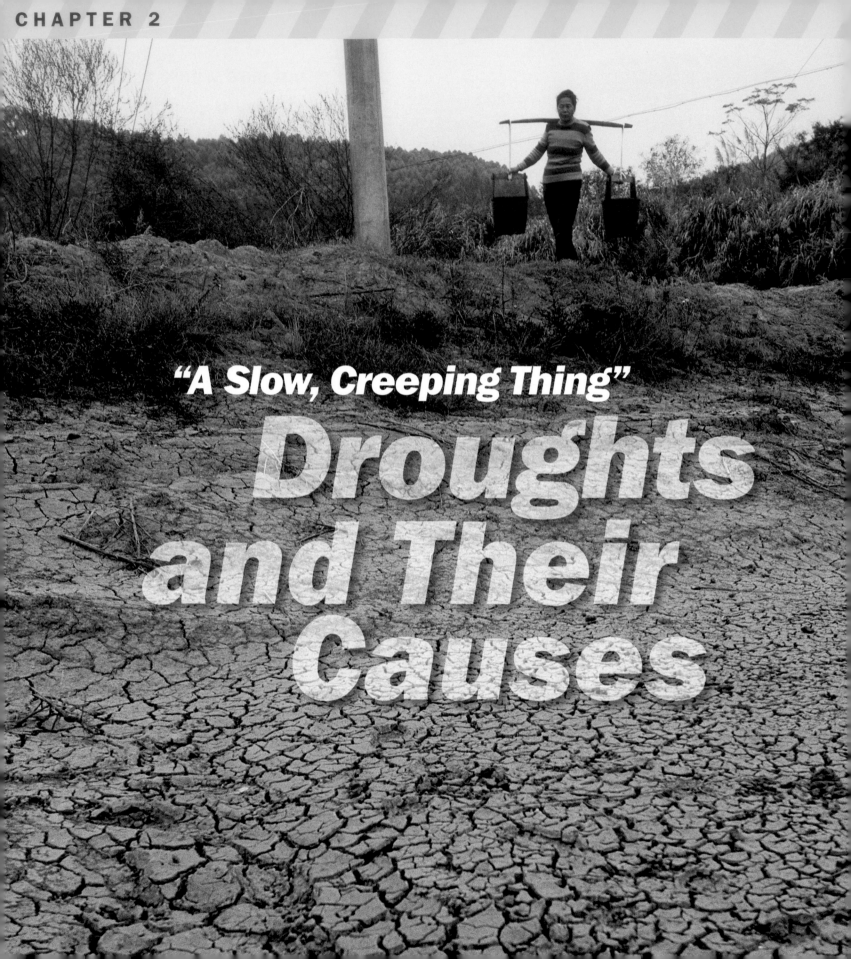

CHAPTER 2

"A Slow, Creeping Thing"

Droughts and Their Causes

A satellite view of our beautiful planet shows the oceans and seas that give it the nickname, "The Big Blue Marble."

THE WHAT, WHEN, AND WHY OF DROUGHTS

Perhaps the third planet from the sun should have been named Ocean instead of Earth. Only 30 percent of our planet's surface is land. Seventy percent is covered by water.

"You can have a flood in the middle of a drought and still have a drought going."

Hydrologist **Frank Richards**

Our planet would be lifeless without water, which every animal and plant needs. Water makes up 96 percent of a head of iceberg lettuce, 84 percent of an apple, 74 percent of a banana, 70 percent of an elephant, and 65 percent of a mouse or a human being. Water comprises 82 percent of your blood and 70 percent of your brain.

Earth's water originated when our planet was young. Since then, no new water has been created, and none has disappeared. Our planet always has the same amount of water. The water you washed your hands with today might have been bathwater for Ben Franklin more than two centuries ago, or drunk by dinosaurs 150 million years ago. Your great-great-grandchildren may swim in it a hundred years from now.

Earth has about 325,000,000,000,000,000,000 (325 quintillion) gallons of water, scientists figure. That sounds like a lot, but 97 percent of it is ocean saltwater. To survive, human beings and many other living things depend on the other 3 percent—freshwater.

During a devastating drought in 2005, this woman from the southeastern coast of China had to carry water back to her family after local wells and ponds dried up.

Although the amount remains constant, water continually moves from place to place while changing in form between liquid, gas (water vapor), and solid (ice). Called the *water cycle*, the movement of water works as follows:

The sun's heat evaporates or dries up water from lakes, rivers, oceans, and from the soil. (As water evaporates from oceans, the salt is left behind.) In the evaporation process, the water changes from a liquid to a gas form. This water vapor rises high into the air where it can form clouds, which are tiny water droplets or ice crystals. When clouds become heavy with moisture, rain or snow falls from them. The sun's heat evaporates the moisture, starting the cycle anew.

It would be wonderful if every locale always received the water its living things require. That doesn't happen. Sometimes so much rain falls on a region that floods occur. Other times an area may experience a prolonged dry spell, depriving people, plants, and animals of their customary amount of water. Then the region suffers from drought.

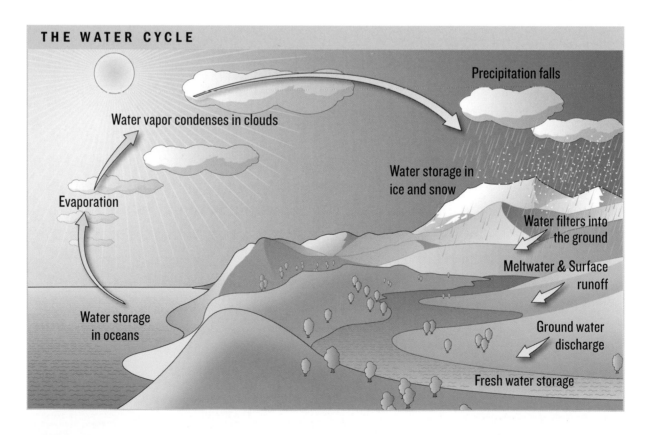

THE WATER CYCLE

Precipitation falls

Water vapor condenses in clouds

Water storage in ice and snow

Water filters into the ground

Evaporation

Meltwater & Surface runoff

Water storage in oceans

Ground water discharge

Fresh water storage

These Somalian women walked six miles into Kenya to scoop water for their families.

"Any place in the world can have a drought," explains climatologist Mark Svoboda. Every area receives a certain amount of precipitation (rain, melted snow, and other kinds of moisture) in a typical year. For example, tropical rain forests average more than 80 inches of yearly moisture. Much of the Great Plains of the United States usually receives about 20 inches of yearly moisture, while deserts average fewer than 10 inches. A tropical rain forest that only received 40 inches of moisture in a year would be suffering from a drought. Even deserts can experience droughts if they go long enough with very little or no water.

> "Weather *refers to day-to-day conditions of the atmosphere.* Climate *refers to the typical weather an area has experienced over many years.*"
>
> Drought specialist **Dr. Donald Wilhite**

SOME IMMEDIATE CAUSES OF DROUGHT

Droughts have several immediate causes. These are the conditions that bring on a prolonged dry period in a particular place.

Many regions depend on the spring snowmelt to trickle down mountainsides, moisten the ground, and provide water for streams and rivers. But what if there is little winter snowfall? Then in the spring when the snow melts,

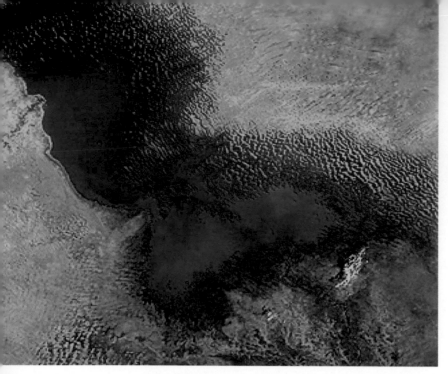
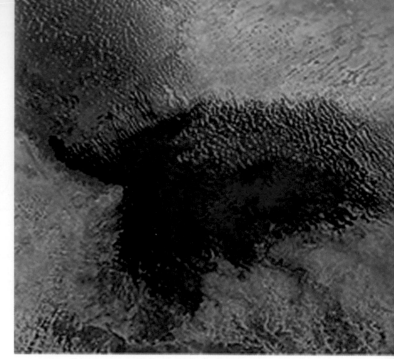

In the 1960s, Africa's Lake Chad was the sixth largest freshwater lake in the world. By 1997, persistent drought had shrunk it to one tenth its former size. The red coloration shows where vegetation replaced open water.

there might not be enough water to grow crops, fill streams and lake beds, or provide water for fish and other animals. Less than normal snowfall contributed to the droughts in the American West in the early years of the 21st century.

Wind is a key factor in many types of weather, including drought. Each part of the world has fairly predictable wind patterns. Sometimes, though, the usual patterns don't hold true. Then rain clouds can miss their usual targets, resulting in drought in one locale and perhaps floods in another. For example, India depends on winds called monsoons to carry summer rains into the country from the Indian Ocean. At times the summer monsoon winds are weaker than usual. The result is less rain than expected.

Meteorologists speak of low- and high-pressure systems. Air exerts a downward push, or pressure, due to the Earth's gravity. When air rises, it creates a system of low pressure. In that case, water vapor rises and forms clouds that produce rain and snow. But when air descends, it causes high pressure. Water vapor dries out, and the result is clear, sunny skies. If a high-pressure system persists over an area for a long time, the region may experience drought. China's droughts at the start of the 21st century were partially caused by persistent high-pressure systems.

High temperatures also contribute to drought. The heat bakes the ground so hard that rainfall cannot penetrate the soil. The heat also causes surface water to evaporate faster than normal, making rainfall disappear quickly.

During mild droughts, people may be asked to limit water usage for household tasks and for lawn care. Should the dry conditions persist, water may be rationed, meaning that everyone can use only a given amount.

In more prolonged droughts, crops and livestock die. Rivers, lakes, and ponds drop in height or dry up completely. Boats cannot deliver life-saving cargo because waterways are too shallow to navigate. Winds whip up topsoil, and carry it off in dust storms. Most regions have only about ten inches of topsoil—the rich, fertile upper layer of soil in which farmers plant their

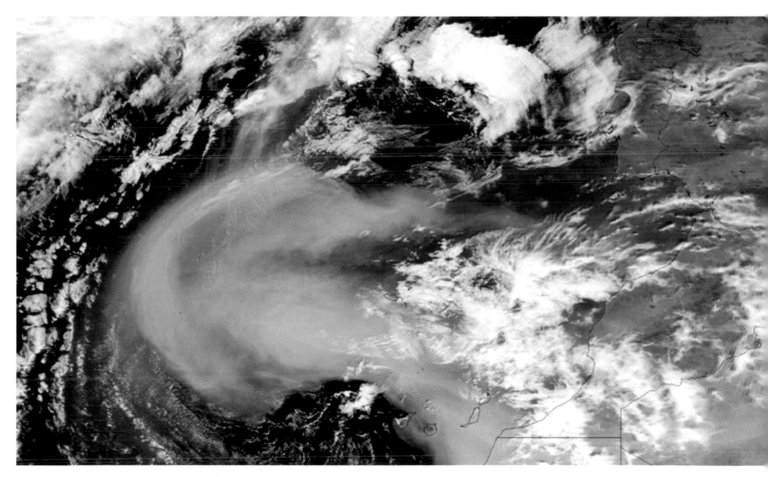

This satellite image taken in the year 2000 shows a huge dust storm blowing about 1,100 miles off the coast of northwest Africa.

LOSS OF TOPSOIL AND DESERTIFICATION

Some scientists have a theory that land with plants and trees might have an increased chance for rain. Plant life blankets the soil, retaining solar heat at night, releasing it during the day. When air containing moisture from the plants rises, clouds form. If the soil is bare because of a loss of topsoil or poor farming practices, this cycle is broken.

crops. It takes roughly a century to form just one inch of topsoil. A single dust storm can blow away much of a farm's topsoil, destroying 1,000 years of nature's work.

The most severe droughts destroy plant and animal life so completely that food shortages occur. The United States and other wealthy nations have enough food reserves to help their people survive years when drought destroys crops. But in poor countries where people have nothing to eat except what they grow, major droughts can result in famines. These periods of widespread hunger are often accompanied by thirst and disease and are the most devastating aspect of droughts. Drought-related famines have killed more people than have all the hurricanes, volcanoes, floods, earthquakes, and tornadoes ever to strike our planet added together.

Droughts also spark fires. Drought was a major factor in two historic fires that occurred the same day: the Great Chicago Fire and Wisconsin's Peshtigo Fire, both of which took place on October 8, 1871. Over a century later, in 1988, fires caused by drought nearly destroyed Yellowstone National Park.

GLOBAL WARMING

Many scientists believe that human activity is making droughts more of a problem. They claim that people are actually changing our Earth's climate through a process known as *global warming*.

When we burn automobile gasoline, natural gas, oil, and coal, we release vast amounts of carbon dioxide gas (CO_2) into our planet's atmosphere. Over the past two centuries, the amount of CO_2 in the Earth's atmosphere has greatly increased. The CO_2 traps heat that would otherwise escape out into space, making our planet a little warmer than it would otherwise be. Human activity also produces other pollutants that prevent heat from escaping. During the past hundred years, the average temperature of our planet has increased by a little more than 1°F.

In the future, we can expect even more dramatic global warming. "Temperatures are expected to rise by another 2° to 6°F by the year 2100," says Dr. Donald Wilhite, founder of the National Drought Mitigation Center in Lincoln, Nebraska.

On October 10, 1871, strong winds fanned the flames of the Great Chicago Fire, which killed hundreds of people and destroyed four square miles of the city.

Many towns and farms use wells and pumps to draw their water from aquifers. These underground reservoirs formed as fresh water seeped slowly through the soil into porous rocks beneath the Earth's surface.

"Problems arise when water is withdrawn from aquifers at a rate greater than can be replenished. As the water level in a shallow aquifer goes down, it may cause water levels in lakes and water flows in rivers to drop, leaving even less water for human use. Worse yet, an aquifer may eventually run out of water altogether, leading to disaster during a prolonged drought. And if the porous rocks of a shallow aquifer are no longer filled by water, the rocks may compress, creating sinkholes in the overlying land."

Dr. Charles Dunning, Assistant Director of the U.S. Geological Survey, Wisconsin Water Science Center

Global warming can be expected to contribute to more severe and more numerous droughts. For one thing, higher temperatures increase evaporation. As a result, less water remains in the soil to grow crops and less water is available for humans. Also, global warming may create changes in ocean currents and wind patterns that affect the amount and distribution of rainfall.

"Global warming will lead to more weather extremes," summarizes Dr. Wilhite. "Some places will get wetter and have more floods. Some will get drier and have more droughts."

> *"Hurricanes and tornadoes and earthquakes and floods have a definite starting and ending time. They hit you— POW!—and then they're over. Droughts are a slow, creeping thing that you don't see coming and are hard to define. You may not even know you're in a drought until it's well underway."*
>
> Meteorologist **Richard Heim**

WHAT CAUSED THE RECENT DROUGHTS?

Why were there so many and such severe droughts at the start of the 21st century? Many climatologists think that global warming caused by human beings has something to do with it. However, they disagree as to how big a role global warming is playing. There are also other ideas about what lies behind periods of widespread drought.

Some climatologists point their finger at the sun as the master control behind droughts. Our planet receives its heat and light from the sun. But our star does not always produce the same amount of energy. When it generates more energy than usual, it heats the Earth a little bit extra, perhaps causing a period of droughts. When our sun produces less energy than usual, our Earth receives less energy, and so it cools off somewhat.

During the 1980s, climatologist J. Murray Mitchell explained his theory that many severe droughts are related to a 22-year cycle involving sunspots and magnetic disturbances on the sun. Dr. Mitchell said that the solar disturbances create changes in the Earth's upper atmosphere. These changes, in turn, cause temporary fluctuations in our climate, including droughts.

Droughts actually have occurred in western portions of the United States roughly every 22 years. For example, the region suffered droughts in the 1930s (the "Dirty Thirties"), the 1950s (the "Filthy Fifties"), and the 1970s, before the recent prolonged dry spell that began in the late 1990s. However, scientists disagree as to whether it was a coincidence or whether there really is a cycle of severe droughts related to solar activity.

Other scientists claim that some of the droughts of the early 21st century aren't as bad as they seem. They say that a big problem is that too many people have crowded into places that tend to be dry even in the best of times. Explains climatologist Kenneth F. Dewey: "There are increased demands for water—for example in places like Las Vegas, Nevada, and Phoenix, Arizona. Even with so-called 'normal' rainfall, there will be shortages of water in places like these due to increased human demands. The desert will always be a desert, and when we put people into the desert and demand that we have endless supplies of water, it is clearly man's folly."

Much remains to be learned about the various phenomena that trigger droughts. This research is very important, for as the next chapter shows, droughts have caused some major disasters.

Las Vegas, Nevada, is still one of the fastest growing cities in America. Mega-houses, green grass lawns, and artificial ponds are a remarkable—and unsustainable—addition to the original desert landscape.

CHAPTER 3

"Is This the End of the World?"
Some Deadly Droughts

A massive roller slammed into Hooker, Oklahoma, on June 4, 1937.

Paleoclimatologists try to discover weather patterns over thousands of years.

HOW DO WE LEARN ABOUT DROUGHTS?

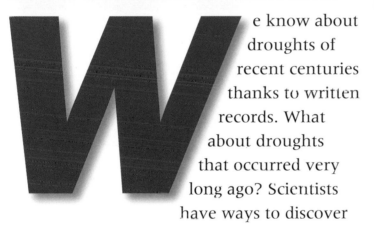

We know about droughts of recent centuries thanks to written records. What about droughts that occurred very long ago? Scientists have ways to discover some basic facts about these weather disasters. The study of ancient climates is a science called *paleoclimatology*.

"The world is warming, and it is foolish to pretend that it's not."

Paleoclimatologist **Lonnie Thompson**

For example, a tree grows a new layer of wood each year of its life. These layers appear as *tree rings* within a tree's trunk. Thick rings grow during years of plentiful rainfall but the rings are thin when rainfall is sparse. By analyzing the ring patterns of very old trees, paleoclimatologists reconstruct what a region's weather and climate were like centuries or even thousands of years ago. Sometimes they analyze the rings from dead trees buried in the ground or submerged underwater. When studying living trees they use an *increment borer* to extract a core sample of wood. This tool does not harm the trees yet provides the tree-ring samples the paleoclimatologists seek.

Sediments (layers of mud, sand, and gravel) also provide clues about past conditions. Over time, sediments settle on lake bottoms. Paleoclimatologists collect samples of old sediments. One thing they look for in the sediment samples are parts of plants called pollen grains. What if the climate detectives

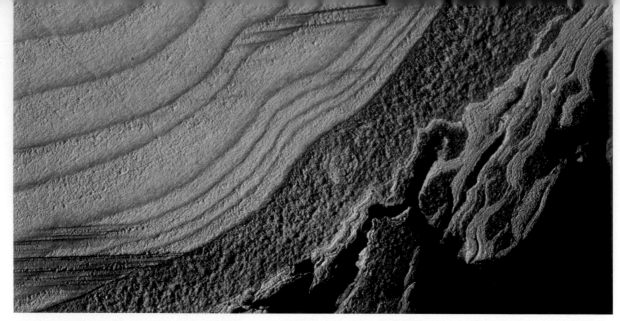

The four narrow rings on the outer edge of this tree trunk indicate four years of drought.

find pollen grains from desert plants in 1,000-year-old lake bed sediment? Then they know that ten centuries ago the area was dry. But if they find pollen grains from plants that grow in climates with lots of moisture, they know that 1,000 years ago the region had a wet environment.

A FEW ANCIENT DROUGHTS

Droughts occurred long before there were people on Earth. More than 12,000 dinosaur bones have been found in Utah's Cleveland-Lloyd Dinosaur Quarry, which was apparently the site of a Jurassic watering hole. Most of the bones are from large, meat-eating dinosaurs called Allosaurus. Why did so many dinosaurs die in the same place 147 million years ago? Recent sediment studies suggest that they may have died as a result of drought.

Forty-three hundred years ago, the world's first empire was begun in Mesopotamia, which today is mostly in Iraq. Known as the Akkadian Empire, it collapsed after about a century. Studies of soil samples reveal that a severe, prolonged drought was to blame.

Around the time that the Akkadian Empire was starting, the Maya Indians began to establish themselves on the other side of the world. After flourishing in present-day Mexico and Central America for many centuries, the Mayan civilization collapsed between A.D. 800 and 900. During the mid-1990s, paleoclimatologists found clues in lake sediment indicating that drought destroyed the Mayan civilization.

DEADLY DROUGHTS AND FAMINES OF RECENT CENTURIES

Over the past few centuries, China, India, Russia, and parts of Africa have suffered many of the deadliest drought-related famines.

No country has suffered from droughts as much as China, where it was once believed that a god resembling a dragon caused these disasters. Written records reveal that China experienced 1,015 droughts between A.D. 620 and A.D. 1619—an average of one per year. Because of frequent and severe food shortages brought on by droughts, China has been called the "Land of Famine." Between 1876 and 1879, portions of what is now eastern China received little rain. Crops dried up in a 300,000-square-mile section of the country—an area larger than the state of Texas. By the end of 1879, as many as 13 million people had perished. This may have been the deadliest natural disaster of any kind in human history.

THE DUST BOWL OF THE U.S.

Probably the best-recorded drought in history occurred in the U.S. more than 70 years ago. There are still elderly Americans who remember living through the Dust Bowl years.

Between 1930 and 1936, Maine and Vermont were the only two of the 48 states that escaped drought. In the Great Plains—a vast, grassy area stretching for 2,500 miles across the midsection of the U.S. and a portion of Canada—it looked like a giant dragon had breathed fire across the land. Wheat and other crops withered. Cattle bones littered the parched earth. Poverty and hunger afflicted thousands of families. And there were the dust storms.

On May 9, 1934, powerful winds sucked up dirt from Wyoming

The 1909 drought and famine in China was one of the deadliest disasters of the 20th century. In this photo, Chinese soldiers supervise the distribution of food for famine relief.

and Montana. Moving east, the huge churning cloud scooped up more dirt, filling the sky with 350 million tons of dust. For four days the dust storm tore through the Great Plains and points eastward, turning day to night as it passed.

Motorists, driving along suddenly invisible roads, crashed their cars. People got lost on their own farms. Dust fell on Chicago, darkened skies over New York and Baltimore, and entered the White House in Washington, D.C. Dust even fell on ships in the Atlantic Ocean—300 miles from shore and 2,000 miles from where the dust storm had originated. Back on the Great Plains, millions of acres of crops had been destroyed.

Drought and dust barraged the Great Plains so relentlessly during the 1930s that the decade was called the *Dirty Thirties*. The dust storms were called *rollers* because they rolled in like huge dark clouds, and *black blizzards* when they caused almost total darkness. The drought-stricken portion of the Great Plains that suffered especially terrible dust storms—including parts of Kansas, Colorado, New Mexico, Texas, and Oklahoma—was nicknamed the *Dust Bowl*.

In some rollers, winds reached 100 miles per hour. The winds sometimes lifted dust four miles high and transported it 3,000 miles. Dust storms lasted hours, days, and occasionally weeks. Flashes of lightning and rumbles of thunder accompanied some rollers.

"Lots of times the dust was so bad we could see it blowing in our living room," explains Gerald Dixon, who lived on a farm near Guymon, Oklahoma, in the 1930s. "When you awoke in the morning you'd see the outline of your body on your bed and pillow where the dust had settled around you."

"People would say, 'Is this the end of the world?'" recalls Sam Howard, who lived on a farm near Headrick, Oklahoma. For many, their world did end. Hundreds, perhaps thousands, of people died during the Dirty Thirties from a variety of breathing problems known as "dust pneumonia."

Hot spells made the drought even worse. In 1936, at least 16 states set or tied their all-time high temperature records. Arkansas, South Dakota, Texas, and Oklahoma recorded temperatures of 120°F. Kansas and North Dakota topped out at 121°F. Approximately 5,000 Americans died of heat-related causes in 1936 alone. Livestock suffered, too. Cattle and other animals died of thirst or hunger, or were smothered by dust.

WITNESSES TO THE DUST BOWL

"One of the largest dust storms came on Sunday, April 14, 1935. I was sitting at a soda fountain. A call came in that a dust storm was headed our way. It looked like a thin line on the horizon that gradually got bigger. When it hit, you couldn't see at all. We called that day Black Sunday."

Jay Stanfield, Guymon, Oklahoma

"The dust and sand piled up so high, our school bus sometimes got stuck in the road. We children had to get out and push the bus over the sand hills."

Jessie Howard Reynolds, near Headrick, Oklahoma

"The dust would blow from the south one day, then from the north the next day, so we'd get the same dust back and forth."

Ingeborg Sogn, Oslo, Texas

"I milked three cows on our farm. When I got to the house, the milk foam on top would be red from the blowing dust."

Wayne Q. Winsett, Elmer, Oklahoma

A farmer and his sons run for shelter in the face of a 1936 Oklahoma dust storm.

Parts of western Canada also suffered devastating droughts, dust storms, and heat waves during the Dirty Thirties. Some Canadian farms were buried by tumbleweeds, which thrive in dry regions. Tumbleweeds piled up against barns and houses as much as 20 feet high.

Unwanted creatures flourished in the Dirty Thirties weather. Dry, hot conditions are ideal for hatching grasshoppers. From 1934 to 1938, grasshoppers devoured crops worth hundreds of millions of dollars in and beyond the Dust Bowl. June Rachuy Brindel remembers an incident from 1935, in Grand Island, Nebraska:

> My sister had a vegetable garden. It was growing well until one day we saw what looked like an approaching cloud. As it came closer, we saw that the sky was full of grasshoppers. We ran inside. Grasshoppers were killing themselves banging against the windows. It took a couple hours before they all passed through. When we went back outside we saw that they had eaten up the entire garden.

To make things worse, the 1930s were also the years of the Great Depression. This period of bank closings, joblessness, and hard times hurt both city and farm families. On the Great Plains, hundreds of thousands of people who could no longer make a living moved elsewhere in search of a better life.

However, the majority of Great Plains people decided to wait out the hard times. Even in the Dust Bowl, about two-thirds of the farm population stayed put. Those who vowed to stick it out were called "stickers." They were also called "the next year people" because they claimed that, "if it rains," next year would be better.

But the late 1930s arrived and still "next year" hadn't come. On April 7-8, 1938, a dust storm accompanied by snow clobbered the Dust Bowl. This was called a snuster—a name coined by combining the words snow and duster. Drifts of dirt and snow from the April 1938 snuster made roads impassable, stranding travelers and schoolchildren.

Finally, "next year" arrived. By 1940 the greatest agricultural disaster the United States had ever suffered—the droughts and dust storms of the Dirty Thirties—had for the most part ended. Sam Howard recalls the joy he felt when the rains finally came:

> I went outside, opened my mouth, and let it rain in. It was quite a time
> for celebration.

CHAPTER 4

"You Know That
It Is Hurting"

Drought
Mitigation

GREAT PLAINS PRAIRIE

This stamp set issued by the United States Postal Service celebrates the lush plants and abundant wildlife that inhabited the nation's Great Plains.

D roughts have occurred in the past and they will occur in the future. But even if we can't prevent droughts, we can mitigate them, or reduce their harmfulness.

"We're not going to get any new water so we have to figure out ways of using what we have more wisely."

Dr. Donald Wilhite

IMPROVED FARMING METHODS

The 1930s Dust Bowl wasn't entirely a natural disaster. It was partly the result of poor agricultural practices.

Before settlers arrived in the 1800s, grasses covered the Great Plains. Their roots held the soil in place. Pioneers who came to farm plowed up the grasses, then planted wheat and other crops. Wheat held down the soil only about a thirtieth as well as had the native grasses. Ranchers let their cattle and sheep graze on the rich Great Plains grasses. Once a locale's vegetation was devoured, the ranchers moved their animals to new grazing grounds. This, too, gradually destroyed the native grasses that held the soil in place.

The Great Plains lost even more grasslands in the 1920s with the widespread introduction of the tractor. Millions of acres of grasslands were plowed, and with each passing year the Great Plains had fewer deep-rooted native grasses. When drought and strong winds came along in the 1930s, the soil was no longer held firmly in place, and it simply blew away.

One tree at a time, China is planting greenbelts in order to reclaim land swallowed up by desert. Four forest belts nearly 1,000 miles long have already been planted.

Since the 1930s, the U.S. has made huge strides in adopting drought-mitigation methods. Many other countries also use agricultural techniques to lessen the harm droughts cause.

Most of the United States' extensive irrigation system was built starting in the Dirty Thirties. Irrigation is the supplying of water to farmland by artificial means. Damming rivers is one common way to obtain irrigation water. Dams block rivers and store the water in artificial lakes called reservoirs. The water is sent through canals and ditches and delivered to thirsty farmland and cities. Severe though they were, the droughts of the early 21st century would have been even more devastating without the irrigation systems developed in the U.S. and other countries. China, for example, has been building large reservoirs for irrigation and flood control.

"Another drought-mitigation strategy," says Dr. Wilhite, "is for farmers to change to more drought-tolerant crops. In Africa, farmers have been growing more millet." Able to survive hot, dry conditions, millet can be eaten by

Spanning a branch of the Yangtze River, China's Three Gorges Dam set a number of records: 1.3 million people were moved in order to build it; 13 cities, 140 towns, and 1,350 villages were flooded by the project. It is the longest reservoir in the world.

both people and livestock. Other crops that hold up well to drought include soybeans, sorghum, and new varieties of corn.

Windbreaks, also called *shelterbelts*, are groups of trees planted in a row. Trees mitigate droughts at least four different ways. They store water, block the wind, hold down the soil, and provide shade. In China in recent years the Gobi desert has been expanding and destroying farmland. China has embarked on a massive windbreak program intended to hold back that desert. Known as the Green Wall of China, the project calls for the planting of a nearly 3,000-mile-

This giant open cistern was rebuilt in the town of Thula, Yemen, in order to provide fresh water for its citizens.

long windbreak by about the year 2074. In recent years Australian farmers have also been planting windbreaks to mitigate droughts.

Catchments are ponds on farms. They capture moisture that falls from the sky and store it for times of need. Ethiopia is one of the countries where catchment ponds are used as a drought-mitigation technique.

Many farmers let some of their land lie *fallow* (idle) each year. With no crops using it, water builds up in the soil. Moisture is then available to crops the following year.

For ages, farmers tilled (plowed) their soil to break it up before planting. *Low till or no till* is a method that is gaining popularity. With "low till," farmers plow the ground a little. With "no till," they drill their seeds right into the ground without any plowing. "The result either way is that more water is retained in the soil and is available for crop growth," Dr. Wilhite explains.

"The soil is also less likely to be blown away by the wind." In India, Pakistan, and Bangladesh, farmers have recently had success using the low till or no till method to grow wheat and other crops.

Terracing and *contour farming* are popular drought-fighting measures used on hillsides. In the first method, farmers build step-like terraces. The terraced slopes hold moisture that would otherwise flow downhill and off the land. Contour farming involves plowing fields and planting crops across and around rather than up slopes. This prevents water from running off when it rains and enables the ground to retain more moisture.

Many of the world's farmers help prevent soil erosion and dust storms by planting *cover crops*. These are crops, such as alfalfa or grass, that both hold down and enrich the soil.

OBTAINING MORE WATER

There are several ideas for obtaining more water where it is needed. A drought-mitigation technique that has been used for a number of years is cloud seeding, also called rainmaking. Certain chemicals inserted into clouds can increase the amount of rain they produce. The chemicals are released into the clouds by airplanes or shot into the clouds by ground-based rocket launchers and other big guns. In the first years of the 21st century, Chinese government rainmakers flew 3,000 cloud-seeding missions and fired huge amounts of *cloud-seeding* chemicals from their "rain cannons." Reportedly these efforts have resulted in huge amounts of rainfall.

Cloud seeding is not a cure-all, however. For one thing, clouds must be present for it to work, which is often not the case during droughts. Also, cloud seeding can cause rain to fall in one place that might otherwise fall elsewhere if nature took its course. In China, cities have argued over cloud seeding, accusing each other of "cloud theft."

Although human beings can't survive on seawater, the salt can be removed from seawater to make it drinkable. This desalting process is called desalination. It is achieved by boiling seawater and by several other methods. Desalination has been done for centuries, but during our current era of widespread drought, it has become more popular than ever. As of 2008,

A woman in north central China carries snow to a watertight cave for storage. The desert region in which she lives has no wells, so melted snow is her main source of water.

about 15,000 desalination plants were operating worldwide. Saudi Arabia is the leading country for desalting water. Other countries using desalination include Israel, the U.S., Australia, India, Russia, and Japan.

One problem with desalination is that it is costly. Another is that it is useful for countries near the ocean but not so useful for nations far from saltwater. The desalination process can also harm sea life and create pollution. If scientists can solve these problems, desalination may come into much wider use.

USING OUR WATER RESOURCES MORE WISELY

There is yet another way to mitigate droughts and water shortages. We can use the water nature provides us more efficiently. Making wise use of our water supply is called *water conservation*.

In the past, farmers in the U.S. and many other countries predominantly used inefficient watering systems that flooded large surface areas or threw water up into the air. Much of the water was lost through evaporation. "New sprinkler systems send the water straight down toward the plants," says climatologist Mark Svoboda. "The water goes directly where it is needed and is less prone to evaporation, making for less waste."

Continues Svoboda: "In Africa and Mexico many people collect rainwater in cisterns or catchers. They boil the water and use it for most of their household needs." In Australia, adds climatologist James Risbey, "Many people are buying water tanks, which are fed with rain runoff from their roofs to supplement their water supply."

Using "graywater" is a water conservation technique that holds promise. Graywater is wastewater left over from bathtubs, showers, clothes washers, and bathroom sinks—just about all the water in a home except from toilets. The graywater can be collected and then used for such tasks as watering lawns and trees—but not for drinking. Graywater usage conserves the supply of fresh water.

"You don't have to be grown up to make a difference in conserving water," says climatologist Kenneth F. Dewey. "Fourth graders can tell their parents they don't need to water their lawns every day. They can help plant

A BIZARRE IDEA

One scheme for obtaining more water involves icebergs. Icebergs are composed of frozen fresh water, so theoretically they could supply water for drinking and for farming. Icebergs weighing two billion pounds or more would be wrapped in giant bags to keep them from melting, then towed by boat and floated along ocean currents to countries that are desperate for water. Pipelines could be built that would transport the water from coastal landing points to inland locations. Fifty or a hundred years from now, will part of the world's population be drinking melted icebergs?

This photograph shows a trawler dragging an iceberg away from an oil rig. Oil companies no longer attempt this risky and dangerous feat.

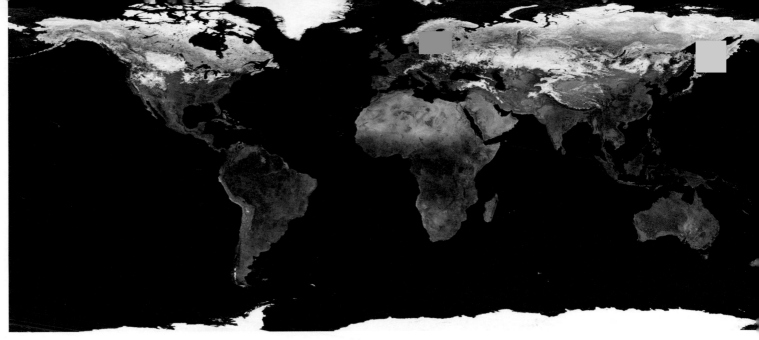

In this April 2005 satellite image, the light brown areas are in the midst of extreme drought.

vegetation that will shade their houses and lawns." There are many other things that every family can do to conserve the planet's water supply. These range from flushing the toilet less often to taking shorter showers.

SAVING PEOPLE FROM DROUGHT-CAUSED FAMINES

Much can be done to mitigate the drought-related famines that have always plagued poor countries. Satellites are a key component of such efforts. "When you look at a satellite picture and the vegetation is browner than normal, you know that it is hurting," explains meteorologist Richard Heim. "You need more information to determine if it's being caused by a drought. The United States has helped many nations establish weather stations on the ground." Between the satellite images and the weather stations, scientists can determine if an area is suffering from a drought that may lead to a famine.

Organizations such as the United Nations World Food Program use the data to identify and assist areas at risk for famine due to drought. They alert people about possible famines and bring in food to try to head off a disaster. These are critical steps toward combating one of humanity's oldest foes: the blue-sky killer known as drought.

"The people who move to the West today need to realize they're moving into a desert."

Pat Mulroy, Southern Nevada Water Authority

"The frog does not drink up the
pond in which he lives."

–An American Indian saying

Glossary

agricultural—related to farming or ranching

black blizzards—nickname for especially severe dust storms that bring on extreme darkness

catchments—ponds for storing rainwater and other moisture

climate—the typical or average weather for an area determined over many years

climatologists—scientists who study climate

conservation—the act of taking proper care of or preserving a natural resource such as soil or water

cover crops—crops planted to conserve and enrich the soil

cycles—events that occur at fairly regular intervals

deserts—dry regions that typically receive less than 10 inches of moisture per year

drought—a prolonged period when an area's rainfall is well below normal or average

Dust Bowl—a region, including parts of Kansas, Colorado, New Mexico, Texas, and Oklahoma, that was especially hard-hit by the 1930s dust storms

dust pneumonia—a term for a variety of breathing problems caused by dust

dust storms—whirlwinds carrying large amounts of loose sand and dirt over long distances

erosion—the process by which soil and rock are removed by water or wind and moved to different locations

evaporation—the process by which water is converted into vapor, or, as people commonly say, "dried up"

fallow—farmland left unused during the growing season to accumulate moisture in the soil

famine—an extreme lack of food, sometimes caused by droughts

fresh water—water that is not salty

global warming—the theory that air pollution is raising Earth's temperature, which may result in unusual weather including more droughts, floods, and hurricanes

hydrologists—water scientists

irrigation—the process of bringing water to dry places by building dams, canals, and other man-made methods

mitigation—*the process of making something less harmful, often by taking action in advance*

monsoons—*winds that usually help create two distinct seasons for southern Asia – a cool, dry season and a warm, wet season*

pollutants—*substances that dirty Earth's air, water, and land*

precipitation—*rain, melted snow, and other forms of moisture*

reservoirs—*artificial lakes created by damming streams or rivers*

sediments—*layers of such materials as mud and sand, often deposited by water and wind*

shelterbelts (or windbreaks)—*barriers of trees intended to protect farms and land from wind damage*

snusters—*dust storms accompanied by snow (the name was coined by combining the words snow and dusters)*

terracing—*the process of building step-like terraces on slopes to retain moisture*

topsoil—*the upper layer of fertile soil, in which crops are planted*

tropical rain forests—*forests in warm regions that typically receive more than 80 inches of rain per year*

water cycle—*the circulation of water from the Earth to the sky and back to the Earth*

weather—*the day-to-day condition of the air in regard to such factors as wind, heat, and moisture*

When you have little water, every drop is too precious to waste. This man in Australia is scooping runoff out of the street.

Further Reading and Research

FOR YOUNG READERS

Chambers, Catherine. *Drought*. Chicago: Heinemann, 2001.

Coombs, Karen Mueller. *Children of the Dust Days*. Minneapolis: Carolrhoda Books, 2000.

Cooper, Michael. *Dust to Eat*. New York: Clarion, 2004.

Meltzer, Milton. *Driven from the Land: The Story of the Dust Bowl.* New York: Benchmark Books, 2000.

SOME WEBSITES TO EXPLORE

For information about drought especially for kids from the National Drought Mitigation Center:

http://www.drought.unl.edu/kids/index.htm

For information on global warming for kids:

http://tiki.oneworld.net/global_warming/climate_home.html

For hints on water conservation:

http://www.monolake.org/waterconservation/

For information and maps relating to developing famines in a number of countries:

www.fews.net/

A thirsty lion waits his turn as elephants drink at a watering hole in Botswana, southern Africa.

Bibliography

Allaby, Michael. *Droughts*. New York: Facts On File, 1998.

Ammende, Ewald. *Human Life in Russia*. Cleveland: John T. Zubal, 1984 (reprint of 1936 edition).

Bonnifield, Paul. *The Dust Bowl: Men, Dirt, and Depression*. Albuquerque: University of New Mexico Press, 1979.

Bryson, Reid A., and Thomas J. Murray. *Climates of Hunger*. Madison: University of Wisconsin Press, 1977.

Davies, R.W., and Stephen G. Wheatcroft, editors. *The Years of Hunger: Soviet Agriculture, 1931-1933*. New York: Palgrave Macmillan, 2003.

Hurt, R. Douglas. *The Dust Bowl: An Agricultural and Cultural History*. Chicago: Nelson-Hall, 1981.

Johnson, Vance. *Heaven's Tableland: The Dust Bowl Story*. New York: Farrar, Straus, 1947.

Lookingbill, Brad D. *Dust Bowl, USA: Depression America and the Ecological Imagination, 1929-1941*. Athens, Ohio: Ohio University Press, 2001.

Loveday, A. *The History & Economics of Indian Famines*. London: G. Bell and Sons, 1914.

Mallory, Walter H. *China: Land of Famine*. New York: American Geographical Society, 1926.

Mishra, H.K. *Famines and Poverty in India*. New Delhi, India: Ashish Publishing House, 1991.

Newman, Lucile F., editor. *Hunger in History*. Cambridge, Massachusetts: Blackwell, 1992 (reprint of 1990 edition).

Patenaude, Bertrand M. *The Big Show in Bololand: The American Relief Expedition to Soviet Russia in the Famine of 1921*. Stanford, California: Stanford University Press, 2002.

Von Braun, Joachim, Tesfaye Teklu, and Patrick Webb. *Famine in Africa: Causes, Responses, and Prevention*. Baltimore: The Johns Hopkins University Press, 1999.

Worster, Donald. *Dust Bowl: The Southern Plains in the 1930s*. New York: Oxford University Press, 1979.

Interviews

DROUGHT SURVIVORS

Dirty Thirties U.S.

June Rachuy Brindel

Gerald Dixon

Mary Drake

Octava Drury Felty

Frances Herron

Sam Howard

Jessie Howard Reynolds

Ingeborg Sogn

Jay Stanfield

Wayne Q. Winsett

Africa

Zenash Beyene

Cecil Cole (interviewed in 1980s)

Australia

Pippa Smith

SCIENTISTS

Kenneth F. Dewey, Professor, Applied Climate Science, School of Natural Resources, University of Nebraska-Lincoln, Lincoln, Nebraska

Richard Heim, Meteorologist with NOAA's National Climatic Data Center, Climate Monitoring Branch, Asheville, North Carolina

Dr. J. Murray Mitchell, Senior Research Climatologist, NOAA (interviewed in 1980s)

Frank Richards, Office of Hydrology, NOAA, National Weather Service, Silver Spring, Maryland

James Risbey, Centre for Australian Weather and Climate Research, CSIRO Marine and Atmospheric Research, Hobart, Tasmania

Mark D. Svoboda, Climatologist, National Drought Mitigation Center, University of Nebraska-Lincoln, Lincoln, Nebraska

For alerting them to possible links between droughts and dinosaurs, the authors also thank their grandson, Aaron Bernard Todd Fradin.

CONSULTANT

Dr. Donald A. Wilhite, Founder and former Director, National Drought Mitigation Center, School of Natural Resources, University of Nebraska-Lincoln, Lincoln, Nebraska

Broken Hill is a desert town in what Australians call "the sunburnt country"—western New South Wales. During the 2002 Australian drought, this man repaired one of the windmills that pumps water for his ranch.

What Can You Do?

10 WAYS KIDS CAN CONSERVE WATER

1. Don't flush the toilet unless it's necessary. Water conservationists have a saying: "IF IT'S YELLOW, LET IT MELLOW. IF IT'S BROWN, FLUSH IT DOWN."

2. When taking a bath or shower, don't use more water than you actually need.

3. If you use a clothes washer, make sure it's well filled before turning it on. Running numerous small loads wastes water.

4. Doing lots of small loads in dishwashers also wastes water. So if you have a dishwasher, make sure it's well filled before running it.

5. Water grass or flowers in the late afternoon so less water evaporates and more soaks into the earth.

6. Make sure to completely turn off water faucets when you're done using them. Even a small drip can add up to a lot of waste.

7. Don't leave the water running when brushing your teeth. Turn it on only when you actually need it.

8. Many people turn on water and then walk away for one reason or another. Doing so is wasteful. Turn it off!

9. If you see your family members and friends wasting water, tell them about it. It's your world, too!

10. Know that when it comes to protecting the world's water, if you're not part of the solution, you're part of the problem!

If you have a question about droughts, or if you want to talk about droughts, feel free to contact the authors. Dennis and Judy can be reached at: fradinbooks@comcast.net

Index